CW00797798

To........................

From....................

Purple Ronnie's

Little Book to say

I ♥ YOU

First published 2011 by Boxtree

an imprint of Pan Macmillan, a division of Macmillan Publishers Limited

Pan Macmillan, 20 New Wharf Road, London N1 9RR

Basingstoke and Oxford

Associated companies throughout the world

www.panmacmillan.com

ISBN 978-0-7522-2724-5

Copyright © Purple Enterprises Ltd, a Coolabi company 2011

All rights reserved. No part of this publication may be
reproduced, stored in or introduced into a retrieval system, or
transmitted, in any form, or by any means (electronic, mechanical,
photocopying, recording or otherwise) without the prior written
permission of the publisher. Any person who does any unauthorized
act in relation to this publication may be liable to criminal
prosecution and civil claims for damages.

9 8 7 6 5 4 3 2 1

A CIP catalogue record for this book is
available from the British Library.

Printed and bound in Hong Kong

'Purple Ronnie' created by Giles Andreae. The right of Giles Andreae and Janet Cronin
to be identified respectively as the author and illustrator of this work has been asserted by them
in accordance with the Copyright, Designs and Patents Act 1988.

Visit **www.panmacmillan.com** to read more about all our books
and to buy them. You will also find features, author interviews and
news of any author events, and you can sign up for e-newsletters
so that you're always first to hear about our new releases.

a poem to say

I Love You

I sometimes snore at
bedtime
My socks are always smelly

I leave the seat up in the loo

And watch too much on
telly

I hate to do the washing
I'm a rubbish cook, it's true
But one thing that I'll always be
Is so in love with you!

a poem about

Being With You

Some people love watching
football
And some like to play with
their cat
But my favourite thing
Is just being with you
And it's really as simple as
that

a poem about

Bedtime fun and Games

Some couples play at chess
and cards
Or so I've heard it said.

But I prefer the kind of
games
We play when we're in bed!

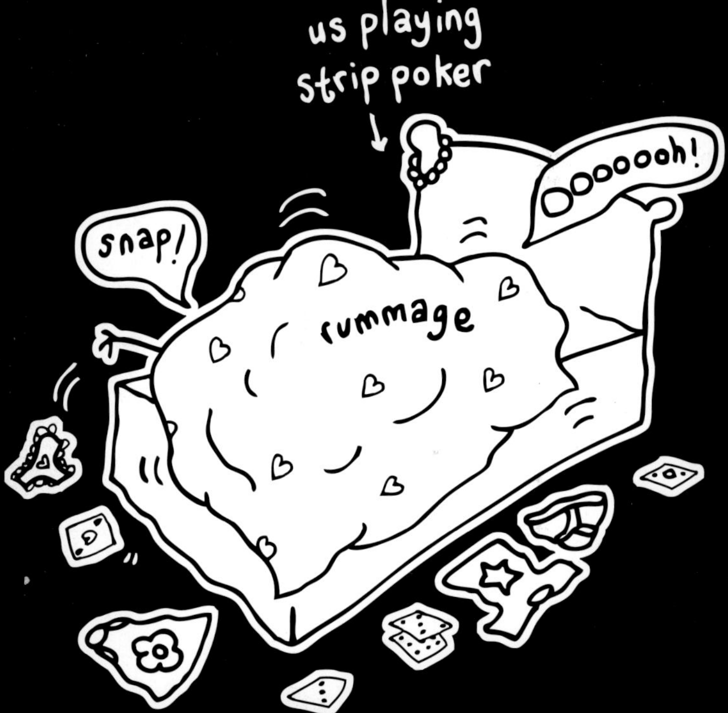
us playing
strip poker
Oooooooh!
snap!
rummage

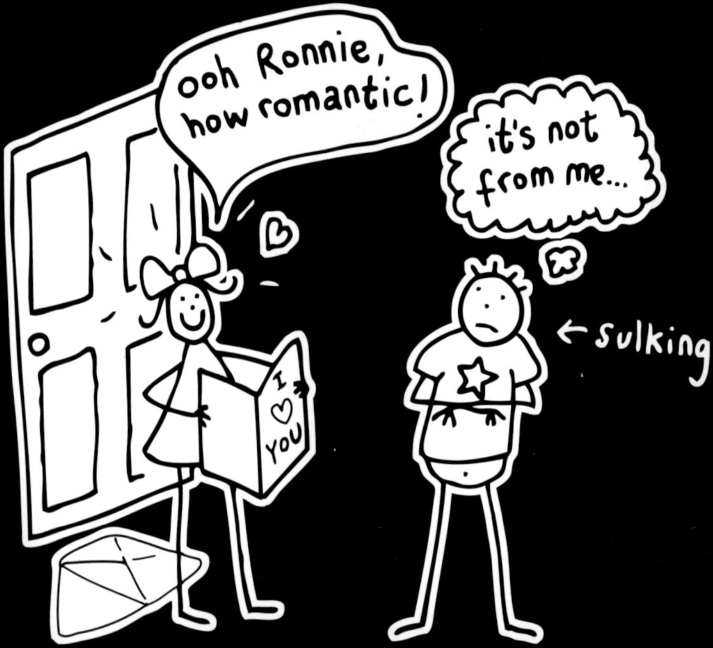
ooh Ronnie, how romantic!
it's not from me...
← sulking
I ♡ YOU

Valentine Cards - 1

Some people like to send secret Valentine cards. This could cause problems.

a poem about

My Scrumptious Lover

You're so unbelievably
gorgeous
I thought that I'd just
have to say
I'd love to submerge you in
chocolate
And lick it off slowly all day!

a

Snuggly Poem

I'd like to be a hamster
Or a hedgehog or a shrew
And go into my hidey-hole
To snuggle up with you

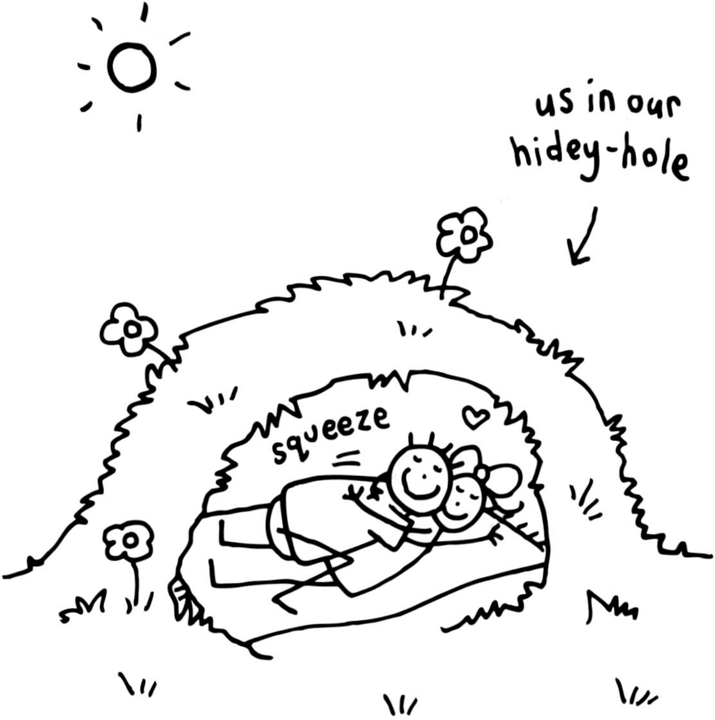
us in our
hidey-hole
squeeze

Cupid's Arrow

Don't be stupid, Cupid.

Stop messing with that
dart,

Oh crikey, I'm so deep
in love -

You've hit me in the heart!

would you like to taste the wine, Modom?
Why, don't mind if I do, don't you know
prrrr

Valentine Dinners

If you can't afford a posh restaurant for Valentine's Night, try a D.I.Y. one at home

a poem about a

Little Devil

My horny little devil
I love you such a lot.
Let's make a love inferno
'Cos devils like it hot!

a poem about a

Superkiss

I'm storing up a Superkiss.
Believe me, yes, it's true.
I'm saving up a Superkiss
Especially for YOU!

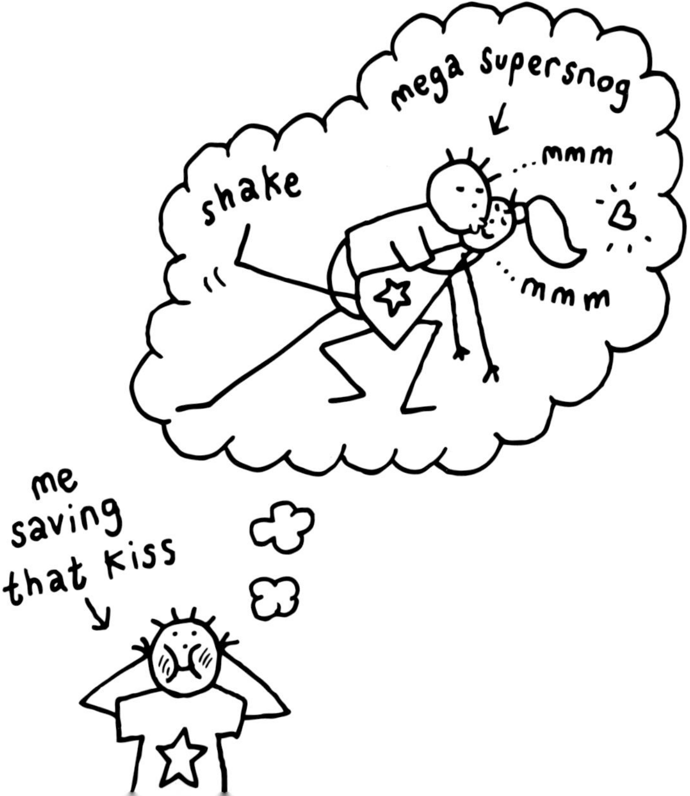
mega supersnog
shake
mmm
mmm
me saving that kiss

a poem about

Heart Strings

'Love is like a violin.'
That sounds just like a
riddle.
Could it mean love makes
us keen
To have a naughty fiddle?

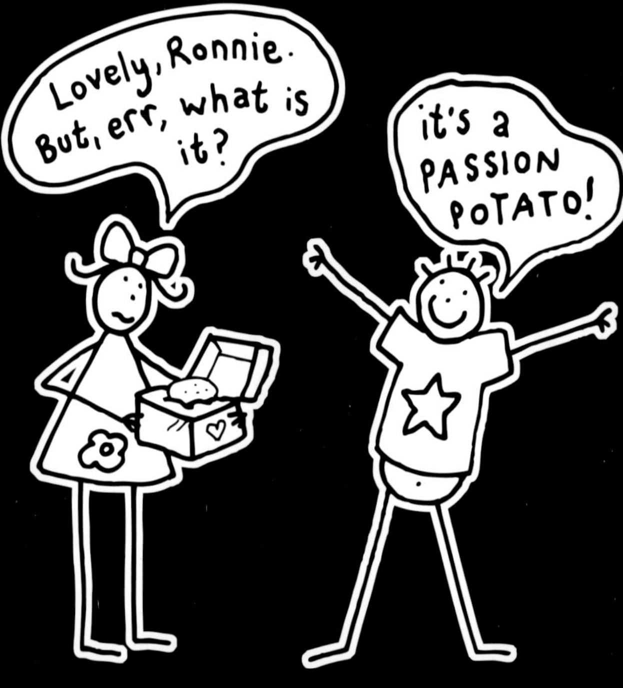
Lovely, Ronnie. But, err, what is it?
it's a PASSION POTATO!

Valentine Presents

Flowers and chocolates are very common Valentine presents. Try sending something a bit more original

a poem about

Body Language

Our bodies speak a language.
What was it they just said?

'Yippee, we're feeling sexy!
Let's snuggle up in bed!'

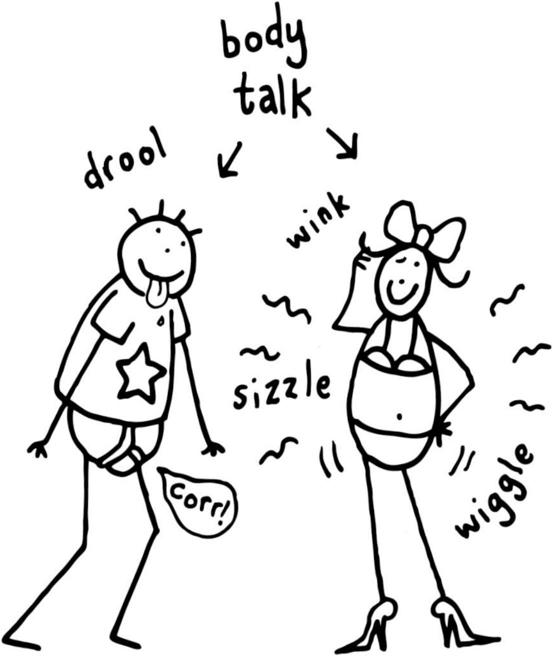
body
talk
drool
wink
sizzle
corr!
wiggle

a poem about a

Meal of Love

Valentine's a sparkling
wine
All pink and sweet and
bubbly.
Let's sip it with some fresh
Love Pie
All steamy, hot and hubbly!

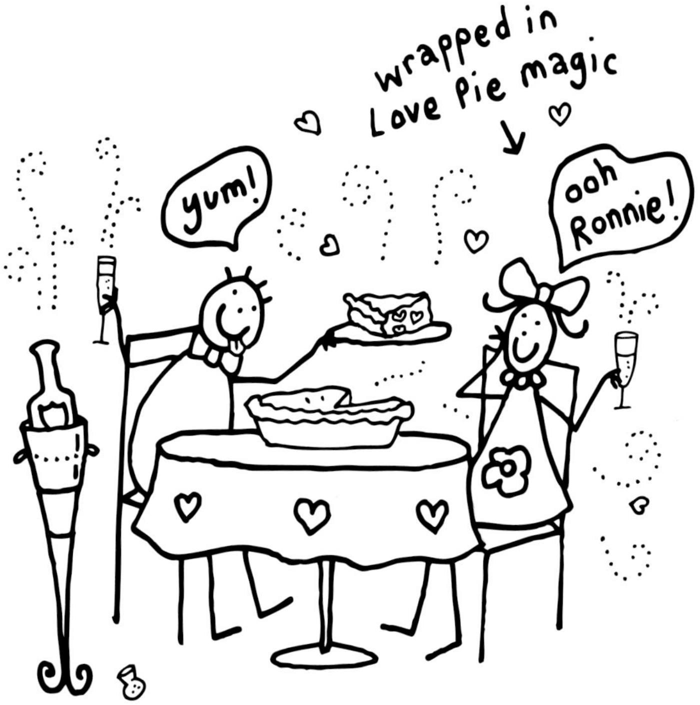
wrapped in Love Pie magic
yum!
ooh Ronnie!

a poem for my
Gorgeous Girlfriend

Here's a little message

For a girlfriend who's the
tops

It's to tell you that you're
gorgeous

And to say I love you lots

Romantic Environments

Some people like to make
a romantic setting for
Valentine's Day

a poem about a

Hunky Heart-Throb

I think it's time to tell you

The way I've always felt

You're such a hunky heart-throb

That my knickers want to melt!

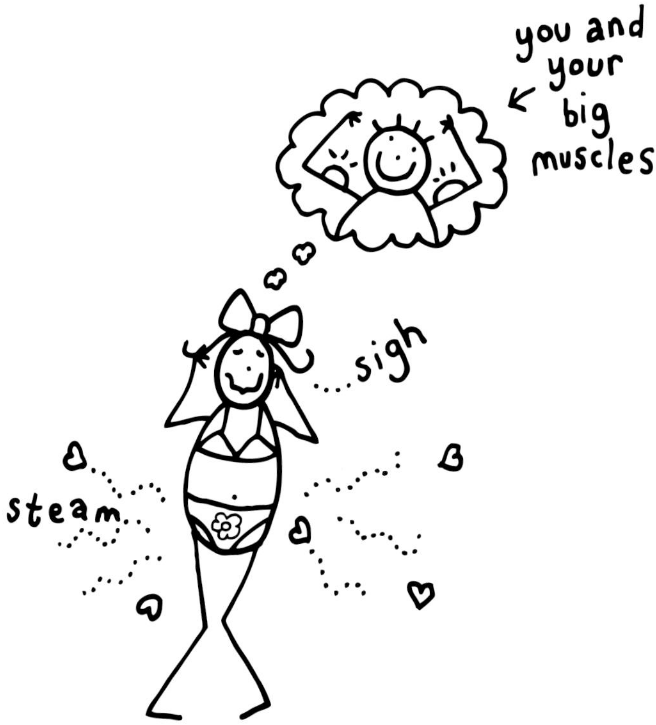
you and your big muscles
sigh
steam

a poem to say

I Love You

I want to tell you something
Now at last I've found a way
I love you more than
                    chocolate
And that's all I need to
                    say!

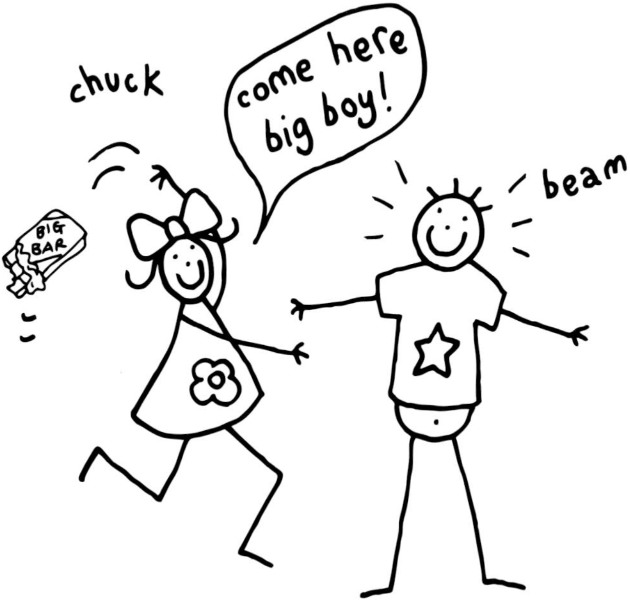
chuck
come here big boy!
beam
BIG BAR

...and that's why I love you
oh, that's lovely, Ronnie. Thank you
my great writing

Valentine Poems

Valentine's Day brings poetry out in some people. Try writing a poem for your loved one.

a poem about

kissing

Some kisses last for just
seconds
They're gentle and go on
cheeks
But I like the ones you put
right on the lips
That can go on for 2 or 3
weeks!

munch slurp

snog

↑
snacks

Valentine Cards - 2

In the past people used
to make their own
Valentine cards for sending.
If you do this make sure
your skills are up to the
job.

a poem for

My Gorgeous Valentine

Here's a little message
For my gorgeous Valentine
It's to tell you that you're
        fab
And I'm so happy that
        you're mine!

a poem about a

Love Spell

Abracadabra! Hocus Pocus!

Ala kazam kazee!

I'll wave my magic wand
and then
You'll swoon when you see ME!

WOW! You look great!
Not so bad yourself hunky
us all dressed up

Looking Good on Valentine's Day

Make yourself good to look at on Valentine's Day. Dress very up.

a poem about a

Sexy Babe

You're scrumptious and
you're sexy
You're fabulous and fun
And I'd like to tell you
something else
You've got a gorgeous bum!

a poem about an

Alternative Valentine

Instead of giving flowers

Why not do some household
chores?

Now THAT could make me
love you

And I'd be completely yours!

a poem about

Loving

It's all very well to be hung
like a hippo
And make ladies squeal
with delight
But sometimes they much
prefer someone who cares
To be holding them closely
all night

Children on Valentine's Day

Some children like to make their mums a Valentine Card to say they love them.

a poem about

Sweet Talk

You're my little cup cake
With a cherry on the top.
Once I've started nibbling
you
I simply cannot stop!

a poem to say

I Love You

I may not always say it
But I promise you it's true
I love you, you're amazing

And I think the world
of you